MW00559364

This book belongs to

Charlotte

This book is dedicated to my children –
Mikey, Kobe, and Jojo.

Copyright © 2020 by Grow Grit Press LLC.
All rights reserved. No part of this book
may be reproduced in any form without
permission in writing from the publisher.
Please send bulk order requests to
growgritpress@gmail.com
978-1-63731-048-9
Printed and bound in the USA.
GrowGrit.co

Mae Jemison

By Mary Nhin

Pictures by
Yuliia Zolotova

Hi, I'm Mae Jemison.

As a child, I dreamed
of going into space.

I loved all things science and was
frustrated to see that there were no
women astronauts when I was a girl.

My parents encouraged me to chase my dreams.

But not everyone believed in me.

Girls can't do that.

Stop dreaming, Mae.

I was good at dancing too. I'd taken classes since I was eight years old, and I was a cheerleader at high school.

It was much easier to get support as a young woman wanting to be a dancer than it was as a young woman scientist.

When I graduated from college, I wasn't sure what I wanted to do. I could go back to dancing or go to medical school. But what I really wanted was to fly to space.

I'd been discouraged by so many people over the years about my dreams of flying to space. So, I chose the safer route and trained as a doctor.

One day the television was on and the news highlight was astronauts. But they weren't just any astronauts. There was a women astronaut and a black astronaut! I almost fell out of my chair. I couldn't believe my eyes!

Women and people of color could really do it. We can fly to space. I always knew it. Right there and then, my love and dreams were reignited.

I summoned the courage to apply to NASA. And guess what? Out of 2000 applicants, I was one of the 15 chosen!

I worked very hard, but it also helped that I loved my work. I was soon selected for a space flight.

Although I had almost been discouraged from trying, told again and again that I would fail, I kept working towards my dream. My courage and conviction had faltered at times, but my hard work paid off. And in the end, I was brave enough to chase my dreams.

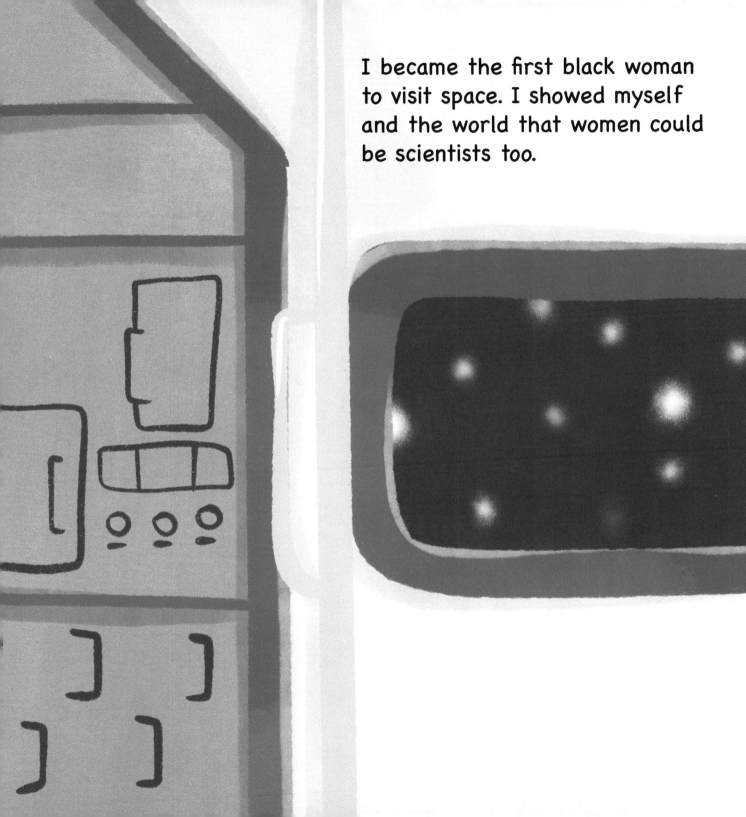

I became the first black woman to visit space. I showed myself and the world that women could be scientists too.

Timeline

1973 - Mae starts Stanford University at the age of 16

1981 - Mae graduates Cornell Medical School

1987 – Mae is chosen for the NASA astronaut training program

1992 - Mae becomes the first black woman astronaut to fly to space

1993 – Mae receives the Kilby Science Award

2004 – Mae is inducted into the International Space Hall of Fame

2017 – Mae receives the Buzz Aldrin Space Pioneer Award

minimovers.tv

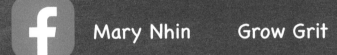 @marynhin @GrowGrit
#minimoversandshakers

Mary Nhin   Grow Grit

Grow Grit

CPSIA information can be obtained
at www.ICGtesting.com
Printed in the USA
BVHW051122021121
620551BV00007B/935